From Fowl Fiascos to Feathered Friends

Learn The Ins And Outs Of Real Life
Chicken Ownership With A Side Of
Redneck Humor

Jenny M. Hendricks

This is a work of nonfiction. No names have been changed, no characters invented, no events fabricated.

Bertha the Very Mean Chicken actually does live at Hendricks Farm in McBean, GA, though she should have been sent to the stew pot long ago for her disgraceful behavior and bad attitude. She has been saved many times by her raving fans, who love to hear about her latest antics.

For more information, email jenny@hendricksfarmhatchery.com.

ISBN Paperback: 979-8-89316-654-5
ISBN Hardback: 979-8-89316-655-2
ISBN eBook: 979-8-89316-653-8
ISBN: Audiobook: 979-8-89316-343-8

Dedication

To my Granddad and Grandma Jacobs, who are no longer here with us. The memories made on your farm each summer will live in my heart forever. I wish that I had spent more time learning about how you raised your chickens, but your warning about using an iron-clad glove lives with me forever, as discussed in Chapter 13.

Contents

Section 5 - Chicks with Attitude

Foreword

I n the world of farming and business innovation, there are inspiring individuals like Jenny Hendricks who stand out. I'm excited to share her remarkable work with you. Jenny's book is more than just a guide; it's like a passport to a world where the clucking of hens teach valuable life lessons, and the pecking order holds secrets that go beyond the chicken coop.

Jenny's storytelling is both relatable and amusing, revealing a personal journey that goes beyond the pages. It reminds us that every venture, whether dealing with feathers or finances, begins with a spark of curiosity. As you read further, you'll discover a tapestry of wisdom woven from Jenny's hands-on experiences.

The lessons in the book go beyond poultry, offering insights into the art of forming alliances— much like coaching a team or cultivating a business. Whether you're an experienced farmer, a curious city dweller, or an entrepreneur exploring new territories, this book is not just about chickens. It's a thoughtful exploration of life's unexpected joys and challenges.

Daniel Hastings
Author, Business Coach, Friend
info@coachdanielhastings.com

Introduction

So you've never had chickens before, eh? Well, just a word of warning before we get started here.

Chickens are the gateway drug to farming. Yeah, it's addicting... very addicting.

I should know. There are chickens everywhere. Tucked here and there and everywhere around the farm. A few enjoy hanging out with the goats soaking in the morning sunshine, while others clean up leftover breakfast scraps from the pig pen, and still others are out on a mission to find bugs under the leaves in the woods. Oh, and now that I'm thinking about it, that field over there looks like another great spot to put even more chickens or maybe a bigger chicken coop. As I said, addicting.

But it also comes with some problems too. Namely, Bertha the Very Mean Chicken.

I am pretty sure that Bertha is working on forming her own coop in an effort to overthrow the farm. Either way, there's definitely some fowl play going on out there in the chicken yard.

Even though I spent summers at my grandparents' farm, I didn't know anything about chickens when I hatched a few baby chicks as an adult. But don't worry, I'll teach you what I learned the hard way, so you know how to handle all the characters from Bertha the Very Mean Chicken to Dwayne the Barred Rock.

Remember that birds of a feather flock together, so once you learn how to handle the likes of Bertha, you'll also be able to handle Peaches, who landed herself in Chicken Jail, as you'll see later. Oh, you don't know about Bertha or Chicken Jail? Well, no fears, because we're going to explain all this in detail soon enough.

Just a word to the wise though, Bertha will seriously peck your eye out or anything else that will draw blood. I'll explain my secret weapon for defending myself against her, so I can still gather her eggs daily. I know she is plotting revenge at this very moment.

Or perhaps you have a runaway chicken, like Estelle. Don't worry. We'll go over the three basic rules that chickens follow to evade capture, so you can outsmart them and bring them home safely (even when doing it solo).

We'll even discuss how to deal with villains like the Masked Bandit, whose sole mission in life is to wipe out your entire flock in the middle of the night simply for the fun of it. And of course, I'll share several other events that could possibly happen (and did go terribly wrong for me!), so you can avoid these pitfalls while having a good laugh at my expense.

Brace yourself. It's going to be a shell of a time!

SECTION I

Getting Started from Scratch

Chapter 1

THE PEEP SHOW

Chirp, chirp, chirp.

I was watching the incubator intently. The eggs inside were actually moving all by themselves. It was exciting to say the least. Even Farm Dog was whining with anticipation. And suddenly, there was a crack in the egg, and the sign of a little beak was poking through. I squealed like a girl. Little did I know *who* was about to hatch.

After waiting for 21 days, the Peep Show[1] was starting. The day I had been waiting for was finally here. I had a dozen eggs in the rotating incubator. I

---

[1]   A group of baby chicks whose tiny peeping sounds mesmerize people to watch them play for hours.

had followed the instructions precisely, turning off the moving tray on day 19, and opening the vent to allow for more humidity.

I was bound and determined to have at least ten beautiful hens that would provide an abundance of eggs. Suddenly, the egg started moving again, and I looked intently as it caught my focus. The baby chick was making progress, but it was way too slow for my liking.

I told Farm Dog that we might as well go get some lunch, as there wasn't going to be much progress anytime soon. Farm Dog, not being one to ever turn down a good meal, was immediately at my heels as I left the room, having fully lost interest in the eggs.

We ate lunch with the sounds of loud chirping in the background, as those babies tried to make their appearance into the world. I decided to make one last check before I took Farm Dog for a fence perimeter check. Still no progress. Were these ladies even going to be able to get out of their shells?

Alas, I had been warned not to help them, but it was so difficult not to help them just a little bit. I mean, what could it hurt anyway, right? But Farm Dog needed to go relieve himself on the far side of the property, as he just refused to go near the house.

So, off we went, and I didn't give another thought to the matter of the incubator. It might be hours at the rate they were going. To my surprise, there was a wet baby chick in the incubator when we returned. I was ecstatic even though I had missed the actual event. If there was a happy dance for baby chicks, that was exactly what I was doing.

But I knew that I couldn't hold the baby chick quite yet, because to remove it from the warm incubator while the chick was wet would give it a chill that could possibly kill it. So, like a new mama watching her baby at the hospital through a glass window, I stared intently at the chick, examining every minute detail. To the chick, I must've looked like a predator who just found its next meal, as Farm Dog and I both were grinning from ear to ear.

Thus, I started my chicken journey with those first few mixed breed babies. Of course, I didn't realize at the time, but from those eggs, Bertha the Very Mean Chicken had made her appearance into the world. But her story—and the lessons she imparted—deserve their own chapter later. For now, just remember that she was named Bertha the Very Mean Chicken for a reason.

After about two days, I realized that only four of the dozen eggs were going to hatch. I was extremely disappointed. But perhaps this was a blessing in disguise, because as much as I had wanted baby chicks, I suddenly learned that I was terrified of being pecked by them. Of course, I was mocked by everyone. Little did I know that my fear was based on intuition of what would be coming with Bertha later.

That's right. One of those two "sweet" baby girls became the infamous Bertha the Very Mean Chicken. For now, just know that she loved being held, especially when close to Farm Dog's face, so she was within striking distance of his nose, which she pecked often without fear of retaliation.

The first time it happened, both Farm Dog and I were caught off guard. I had picked up sweet, innocent, little Bertha, cradling her gently between both my hands in an effort to keep her body warm while her face actively scanned the environment. Little did I know that she was looking for a target for her wrath.

I held her up so proudly for Farm Dog, who is 90 pounds of pure muscle. Bertha showed no fear when his big nose came closer and started sniffing her intently. She waited, and waited, and waited... until suddenly she decided it was the perfect opportunity to strike, and she gave a mighty peck straight onto Farm Dog's nose.

Farm Dog jerked back and stared at her in disbelief. Had she really pecked the almighty Farm Dog? Surely, this was a mistake. Farm Dog approached again, and this time Bertha didn't hesitate to strike him firmly on the nose again. Suddenly, this was war, and Farm Dog was barking and growling at the little pecker.

Farm Dog was no longer happy about this new living arrangement. He wanted those chicks out of "his" house now, though he continually kept going into the office to stick his head into the box, only to be pecked by Bertha again. After a while, it seemed that he enjoyed the attention. Surprisingly, he never once tried to make any of the chicks a quick puppy snack.

As the babies grew, I realized something else. Out of the four eggs, I discovered that two of those four chicks were definitely roosters. Fabio was a ladies' man, and the gentler rooster, while Delicious headed to the dinner table thus living up to his name.

So, with only three chickens remaining, I got a bad case of Chicken Math[2], where I felt the need for more chickens. Yes, this is an insatiable desire for more chickens that never ends no matter how many you have.

Of course, I told myself that I just didn't have enough eggs for breakfast, you know. Nevermind, that they hadn't even started laying yet. It never

---

[2]   *The mathematical phenomenon in which no matter how many chickens you have, it is simply not enough.*

occurred to me that you might receive too many eggs and thus create a whole other problem, but I digress.

I went back and asked for more hatching eggs from the neighbor. At this stage of the game, breed didn't matter. It actually had never crossed my mind. A chicken was just a chicken, right?

Soon, we had moved the chicks onto the screen porch within a small baby size coop, where they could run, play, fly, and sleep. Farm Dog loved watching the continuous "Peep Show" or "Chicken TV" through the sliding glass door with his puppy paws so majestically crossed in front of him. We thought that Farm Dog was going to take right up with our birds as they grew with no difficulties at all.

But as we'll see later, it was not going to be such an easy transition.

LESSONS LEARNED:

- Chicken eggs take 21 days to hatch. On Day 19, the vent should be opened to allow more humidity.

- Do not help baby chicks out of their shell. The struggle makes them stronger. Weak chicks that are helped will usually still end up dying.

- Do not remove wet chicks from the incubator, as it can give them a chill that could possibly kill them.

Chapter 2

CHICKEN ROULETTE

At this point, I decided that I needed more chickens and fast. After all, I still had visions of eggs dancing in my head, so I did the next logical thing to increase my flock size. I headed over to our local feed store... you know the one: Tractor Supply.

Now, it really doesn't matter why you decide to go into this store. Just the fact that you are going to be in the store is enough for you to befall the same fate as what happened to me.

As you are walking into the store, you suddenly hear the sounds of little chirps that stop you in your tracks. That's right, the town's Local Peep Show of beautiful chicks is right in the middle of the store. *GASP!* Your heart starts to race, as you must see the origin of these delightful sounds.

Your eyes glance over to the shiny oval metal stock tanks with the Tractor Supply logo on the side that are conveniently located in the middle of the store. You know that is where they are. Your feet are suddenly moving in that direction.

You scream inside that you need to STOP! But it's no use. The sound of chirps draws you over to the Peep Show in progress.

Don't look, you reprimand yourself. But you have to. There is a crowd gathered around the stock tanks, and you join their ranks. You hear the *oohs* and *ahhs* as people look on at those beautifully stunning chicks.

Suddenly, your hand is reaching in. You must hold one of those delightful chicks for yourself. Once in your hand, you must keep it. Oh, and it needs a friend too.

Someone offers you a box, and you greedily accept it. Putting one, two, three... half a dozen chicks into the box. You don't even know what you are doing as you head to the register, grabbing some starter feed on the way out.

Yep, Chicken Math has officially struck again! And the worst part is that you have no clue how you are going to explain this when you get home.

Never mind that, just tuck them in here and there. Nobody will notice, right? After all, you already have so many.

Or maybe this is your first rodeo? And you have no clue how to raise them, but it can't be all that difficult, right? I mean a chicken is a chicken, right?

True, unless you happen to get one of Bertha's relatives. *Ha!*

But seriously, here's the problem that nobody thinks about. Chickens are a lot like puppies. Sure, you can walk into a pet store and just pick up the cutest one, but some puppies are going to need more exercise than others. Some will want to cuddle more and be clingy, while others will grow to the size of Clifford the Big Red Dog.

But none of that matters when you are standing in front of all those shiny oval tubs of chicks. Oh, you'll want a yellow one and a black one and a white one. You tell yourself that you want a mixed flock, so you can tell the chickens apart and name them—a common rookie mistake that I have made myself.

There's a reason why I suddenly found myself running a hatchery. This is addicting stuff that requires intervention of some sort, though nobody has been able to help me yet after several years and hundreds of chickens.

So instead, let me put my addiction to use and tell you about my two favorite chicken breeds and why I like them for homesteading.

Rhode Island Reds and Barred Plymouth Rocks. Yep, both American chickens.

Together, these two breeds are the perfect combination to keep eggs on the table all Winter long. True that they are both hardy and productive. But I love the fact that when one of these breeds slows down in the Winter, the other breed takes over. Then, when the slower one starts up again, the first one takes a break. Maybe they are communicating through the fence, but this keeps me in eggs all Winter long here in Georgia.

Plus, they are large enough to have as a stewing hen, when they eat more feed then they supply in eggs (about the two year mark). We'll talk about Freezer Camp later, so brace yourself, as it's a harsh reality of homesteading.

Other breeds may be cute and cuddly or even have uniquely colored eggs, but these two breeds are tried and true with being productive birds. Remember, all those unique egg colors—blue, green, pink, etc.—come with a price, as those breeds are usually less productive (ie. laying less eggs per year).

And don't even get me started on temperament... Just the name Bertha the Very Mean Chicken should strike fear in your heart already. If it doesn't, just wait. She'll seriously peck your eye out.

It is important to heed my warning by choosing the right breed for yourself instead of playing the game of Chicken Roulette[3] and ending up with something that you didn't want. This time, we are going to take a look at those annoying little labels on the side of the oval metal stock tanks at Tractor Supply. I know, this is almost as bad as stopping to ask for directions. Yet, here we are.

The first label to watch for is going to be called "Straight Run[4]". Sounds so lovely, doesn't it? This is the most dangerous Chicken Roulette that you can play. It means that these chicks are unsexed. Or as a bonus, it can also be the place where hatcheries throw any extra roosters for the unsuspecting newbie. Normally, "Straight Run" bins do *not* work in your favor. They are cheaper for a reason.

The second label that works more in your favor is called "Pullets[5]". These are female baby chicks. *But* remember that sexing is an art and not a science. Seriously, poultry are harder to sex than puppies. The sex organs just aren't obvious to the average Joe, because they are inside the

---

[3] A dangerous gamble where you spin the wheel of luck and hope for females instead of males.

[4] In reality, it is normal to have at least 50% males in a 'straight-run' bin, as the hatcher did not sex them.

[5] Female hens are called pullets, while male roosters are called cocks.

body without any external signs. Depending on the breed, the accuracy of sexing by a professional can be anywhere from 70% to 90%. So, this means that you can still get a rooster, even though you paid extra for a pullet.

Now here is another way that you can play Chicken Roulette. If you live in the city where you absolutely cannot have a rooster, then it may be better to buy a four month old chicken. But even then, it is not 100% foolproof. Let me introduce you to Sideshow Bob (previously Bobbie).

Bobbie was a beautiful Jubilee Orpington chicken that was hatched on our farm. All the roosters adored her. Seriously, if she could have, she would have been wearing pink dresses, dolling up with makeup, and dousing herself with perfume. She had even started laying eggs before going to her new home, which was the cherry on top to confirm that she was definitely a female.

As we have a "HENsurance[6]" policy on all our older ladies, I received a call from my customer some months later stating that Bobbie had started crowing. I reminded her that sometimes hens can "crow". Yes, that just adds to the fun too, I know. But she said that she was starting to look like a rooster and had stopped laying eggs. I told her to

---

[6]   Similar to other types of insurance, this protects you from the unexpected rooster of Chicken Roulette, allowing you to exchange it for a female hen.

bring "him" by the farm, and I would exchange the chicken.

Much to my surprise, it turns out that she was right! Bobbie had become Sideshow Bob! In the chicken world, there is a 1 in a 1,000 chance that you can start with a female chicken and end up with a rooster. Now, hear me out. I wouldn't have believed this either unless I had seen it with my own eyes.

While this is rare (lucky me), this can actually happen. Now, a rooster will never become a hen, but a hen can become a rooster. Hens are born with two ovaries (one is functioning while the other is not). But when the functioning ovary gets damaged, it switches to the non-functioning ovary, which starts to produce male hormones. It's sorta like "hen-opause", where your aunt suddenly shows up with a mustache at Thanksgiving.

The first sign of this transition is that the hen will stop laying eggs. Now, there are other reasons that a hen can stop laying too, so don't jump to conclusions too quickly. But the second sign of this transition will be starting to develop a nice little wattle and a comb... then some saddle feathers and tail feathers. Then, it will start crowing. Again, I wouldn't have believed it myself unless I had seen it with my own eyes.

Just to make this more fun, when you have two hens, one may appear more masculine than the other, even though they are still both hens. That's why this game is called Chicken Roulette. It's a case of Cock-a-doodle-do or maybe not?

Seriously, your chances are up there in the 99% range that it will be a female, but again... we're talking about Chicken Roulette here. Best of luck to you!

LESSONS LEARNED:

- Straight-run bins are cheap for a reason. They usually contain at least 50% males.

- Sexing chicks is an art and not a science, so even pullet bins may only be 70% to 90% females.

- There is a 1 in a 1000 chance that a female hen's one functioning ovary may stop working and cause her to transition to a male rooster.

Chapter 3

FOWL PLAY

Now, at this point, you probably have noticed that Tractor Supply carries ducks, turkeys and sometimes even guineas. Just so you know, Chicken Math isn't just limited to multiplying chickens in your flock, as there are other fowl you can add too. But a word to the wise, don't get ducks. Just don't. They're nasty.

Before we got chickens, we lived on a different homestead way up in Michigan (don't judge—I'm a Native Texan, not a Yankee). We had the most beautiful, picturesque lawn that sloped downhill away from the house where there was a nice field running out to the forest edge. We would sit on the bench next to our little koi pond, as it was so peaceful. One day, another member of the household suggested that we should add ducks.

Memories of ducks waddling around and quacking at the local parks filled my head. *Ahhh, how sweet*, I thought. That would just be perfect to complete the park-like setting we had going. So, we bought six of these little baby quackers, and we began to watch them grow. They loved playing in the kiddie pool that we set up for them in a confined area.

When the leader of the group took off running, all the rest would follow in a perfect line behind him. It was so stinking cute. We could hardly wait for the day when they were old enough that they could free-range on their own. And that day came sooner than expected. They were all hunting for bugs in the grass, being adorable, as they made their way to the top of the hill.

Then, the leader of the duck clan took off running at an alarming pace down the hill while starting to spread his wings. *How weird*, we thought. Suddenly, he had taken flight. Then the second followed, then the third and so on until they were flying over the four-foot tall fence into the field. The grass had appeared greener on the other side, and they were off to explore it.

Thus, we had to wrangle these quackers up and get them back in the yard. The next day, eight-foot tall deer netting was installed at the bottom of the hill along the four-foot tall fence. As anticipated, they all waddled themselves up to the top of the hill again. The leader began racing down the hill while spreading his wings followed by his tribe.

But this time, as he took flight, he slammed right into the deer netting and bounced backward, eventually hitting the ground. The second one was too close behind and the same fate awaited him too. "Abort, abort!" the third one quacked, as he abandoned the course and flew to the side, landing in the grass. They all appeared confused, especially the first one who was lying dazed on the grass.

They never attempted to "escape" again, but the duck problems didn't end there. I mean, after all, who doesn't have fond memories of feeding ducks in the park as a child?

One day, we were eating watermelon, and the ducks came running up to us. They started to get aggressive until we threw them some watermelon. The dog was annoyed, as she loved watermelon and didn't want to share.

Well, ducks love watermelon, but watermelon duck poop is even nastier than regular duck poop, as it's more like diarrhea. The whole deck was slimed. No more walking barefoot outside. They decided that pooping on the deck was preferable to the lawn, especially after having been fed on the deck. Oh well, just another obstacle to our dream of watching ducks on our beautiful lawn, right?

The next day, after having let the ducks free-range for the morning, we realized something was missing in the backyard. All the plants were gone. Even the hostas were gone. And I mean completely gone. They ate them all the way to the ground. It was so bad that years later after the ducks were gone, the plants never returned. But all the books said that ducks only ate bugs and would leave your plants alone. They were wrong!

But never mind that. These three tiny annoyances could be dealt with for the simple enjoyment of watching them free-range our backyard while the koi swam happily in the small pond. However, the ducks were now getting bored in their No-Fly Zone. The end of summer meant no more watermelon for them, and they had already eaten all the plants to the ground. They now had to find something new to entertain themselves.

So, the next thing that happened was finding an empty pond void of koi fish. Oh, there were a few half-eaten koi left floating on top of the pond that told the story. And the culprits were lying in the sun happily having enjoyed a feast just minutes before. I was upset, to say the least. So, we restocked the koi pond with new fish, and we put a fence around the entire koi pond with deer netting on top. It wasn't attractive anymore, but at least the koi were safe.

Until the ducks got smart enough to break the netting and ate all the koi fish a second time. We put up more reinforcements and added more koi. Our beautiful, picturesque setting was getting destroyed by the ducks. They even viciously chased our late cocker spaniel dog down at one point, who seemed oblivious to the whole event at her age. At least the dog didn't attack them, but I wouldn't have blamed her if she had. I might have even been grateful.

Then, one of our neighbors who also had ducks and had convinced us to get them (needless to say, that he was no longer in my good graces) informed us that we needed to get the ducks ready for winter. Apparently, during the harsh winter months, their feet can actually freeze to the ground in Michigan, and they will tear their feet off trying to escape. Now, I didn't know if this was actually true or not, but it was just the excuse I needed to make duck soup.

So, the neighbor came over and assisted with that first dispatching job to Freezer Camp[7] (dis-

---

[7]   A kid-friendly term for explaining the disappearance of older chickens before they become the special guest at dinner.

cussed in detail later), as we had never done it before. Of course, I cried, and I regretted my decision for a moment. But the ducks did taste fantastic, so I eventually got over it. And I was happy to be able to remove the deer netting from the koi pond. Of course, the plants never grew back and that served as a constant reminder of the ducks until we moved.

Now, there may come a time when you want to spread your wings into other fowl, such as guinea fowl or turkeys. Guinea fowl do really well when raised with chickens, but Guineas rule without a shadow of a doubt. The good news about Guineas is that they do prefer to eat only bugs, and they will leave your plants alone.

As tempting as other fowl may seem, they all have certain needs that must be met. The major one for poultry is having secure housing to keep them safe during the night when predators are out looking for an easy dinner.

LESSONS LEARNED:

- Ducks are not a homestead-friendly addition to your flock. They're nasty! Plus, they can fly over a fence into neighboring yards and cause damage.

- Yes, ducks will eat troublesome bugs, but they don't stop there. They can't resist your prized plants or koi fish.

- Guinea fowl are a better alternative for your chicken flock, as they only eat bugs (and ticks) and not your plants.

SECTION 2

Forming the Flock

Chapter 4

SECTION 8 HOUSING

Your first puppy, your first child, and your first chicken all have something in common. You have no clue what you are doing, and you're both nervous and excited about having this new creature, but you are dreadfully afraid of making a mistake and killing it. So, what do you do?

You go all out and buy the best accommodations possible with full attention to detail and no expense spared. I was exactly the same way with my first chickens.

We spared no expense on our first coop. We spent hours *oohing* and *ahhing* over all the fancy coops that we saw online. Yes, we should have nesting boxes that can be opened from the outside. And it should definitely be tall enough to walk in. Roosting bars? Check! A spacious outdoor run that is reinforced, so predators can't break into our gated community? Absolutely!

Our first coop was decked out (well, minus the deck, though that would have been a grand feature!). We bought some nice (and expensive!) plywood and built a four foot wide by eight foot long coop that was eight feet tall. A nice single sloped roof and a fresh coat of barn red paint just added to its majestic appearance. It had plenty of space to walk around in (for us, not to mention the chickens). And of course, six individual nesting boxes were built into the side, so we could easily gather eggs. I mean, seriously, each chicken needed their own nesting box, right? At this point, how could we not name it at the ribbon cutting ceremony. Thus, we named it Holiday Hen.

But after some time, we realized that it had plenty of flaws that one does not figure out until after owning chickens for a while. At this point, I have often wondered why people keep repeating the same chicken house design, when all these flaws are annoying at best to the chicken owner. And then, it occurred to me. Nobody is willing to admit that they made a mistake.

Well, I am going to admit it, so you can avoid these initial failures in your chicken journey.

For our next coop, we used some scrap building materials and this time, free pallets. Instead of a wood floor, which let's face it, poop just seemed to seep into until it was nasty as all getup, we put a hardware cloth floor on it. This allowed materials of all sorts (if you catch my drift here) to fall through the holes and collect below in what I like to call the "Poop Chute[8]". Now, this is nothing more than a pvc pipe frame screwed together with painter's plastic wrapped around and gray taped together at the seams. Yeah, it's a little redneck, but it works. We deemed this mighty structure Fort Cluck.

To live up to its name, it was painted military green too. But I wasn't quite happy with this design either. You see, somebody (and I won't name any names, but I'll let you take a guess), decided that we would make this coop 12 feet long by four feet wide and only four feet tall. It was *way too long*, and due to the shortened height, it made it too difficult to get to the middle of the coop without bending over and squat-walking inside. Of course, what did he care, since I cleaned the coops? But I digress. His argument was that it held more chickens, which

---

[8] This redneck contraption easily allows for poop to be pulled out of the coop, so it can be collected to be used as compost in garden beds.

we will see later that opinion was flawed too. So, I made some more design changes.

This time, I made the raised base eight feet by four feet. The poop chute was also more manageable for me to pull out and dump to the side at this size. Yep, I collected all that gardener's gold and used it to grow some amazing vegetables, but that's another story. The pallets were used to build the sides, and I used extra boards to fill in the gaps. For the doors, *he* insisted that we continue to use plywood, as *he* insisted that doors made of scrap pallet wood would be too heavy for little ol' me. We would soon learn that all of his brilliant "suggestions" were not helpful and always had to be redone. Of course, *he* would casually forget how he had insisted on the incredible genius of his ideas, but those other stories are shared in our daily emails (sign up at www.HendricksFarmMcBeanGA.com). So, the doors were made out of plywood with a wood frame around the edges. Nesting boxes were simply old milk crates with some hay. As I said, the accommodations had declined considerably by this third round.

But here is the crazy (and somewhat funny) part of this whole thing. The chickens actually liked the old milk crates better than the fancy dancy built-in wood boxes that you see on modern chicken coops. *Plus*, as an added bonus for those who have real-world chickens, you could easily take those milk crates out and hose them down whenever they poop in them. *Oh*, your chickens wouldn't dare do that? Ha! We'll see.

Now, it was time to paint this baby up and give it an official name. So, while at Lowe's[9], I happened upon the discounted paint section. Yeah, every paint store has one, and you can get some really good deals. I hit the jackpot that day, or at least I thought. Outdoor paint in majestic purple. Perfect! I grabbed up the gallon pail and headed to the register with confidence.

Back at the farm, I opened it, and oh, it was everything I dreamed it should be. With each stroke of that paint brush, I was grinning from ear to ear, as that royal purple covered the pallet boards. I went inside to take a break and let my creation dry. A few hours later, I returned to find that it had dried *black*! Oh my goodness! This was terrible! A black coop!

I was so heartbroken that I didn't even want to name it. How completely, utterly ugly it was! But I had chickens that needed a new home, as Fort Cluck was overcrowded at this point. Let's not talk about my chicken addiction that caused the issue. Both these coops went into the same run area, so

---

[9] Every hardware store has a discount paint section caused by employee mistakes or customer returns.

I just went ahead and transferred some chickens that night into the new ugly coop. The next day, they all came out and intermingled. They seemed to be quite chatty that morning.

Well, later that night, to my utmost surprise, I couldn't believe how many chickens had transferred from Fort Cluck to the newly named "Section 8 Housing". They had crammed themselves in there—wing to wing—on the perches and squatting all over the floor and in the nesting boxes. *What the heck?* Fort Cluck was deserted. They had all decided that the new accommodations were so much better than any of the previous coops, and they had *all* moved in. I closed the door for the night with a long sigh and walked away.

Chicken brains at work. That's all I can say. To this day, Section 8 is our most popular housing structure. The moral of this story is not to worry too much about the chicken housing. Of course, make it secure, but the more natural the conditions, the better. And even though a four by eight structure should hold 10-12 chickens, according to human standards, don't be surprised if the chickens tell you that it can actually hold upwards of 50 chickens. *Sigh*

Now, going from four to 50 chickens didn't happen overnight. No siree! Chicken Math was definitely to blame. But, there is a right and wrong way when adding chickens to an existing flock, as we'll see in the next chapter.

LESSONS LEARNED:

- Chickens don't need fancy accommodations to be happy. The structure just needs to be secure, so predators can't break in at night.

- Big box stores like Lowe's have a discount paint section where great deals can be found. Milk crates can be purchased at Tractor Supply along with used pallets too.

- Even though a four foot wide by eight foot long structure should only hold 10-12 chickens, don't be surprised if all your chickens want to stay together in it.

Chapter 5

BAD CHICK CLUB

f you already have some mature ladies in your coop, they aren't going to take kindly to any newcomers. Oh, you thought perhaps they would just greet them with a hug, put their wing over their shoulder, and show them around the coop? Bless your heart!

Unfortunately, even Southern hens do not show any sort of hospitality. In fact, it is quite the opposite on most occasions. They see the youngins arrive and immediately swoop in at a cluckin' rate of speed. The pecking order[10] is alive and well, and these mature hens are not about to lose their status in the flock. And the arrival of a younger woman is *always* competition.

Note that this isn't just limited to younger hens either. One time, when I was a less experienced chicken owner, I decided to start a new flock of beautiful Barred Rock hens, because I could always toss in a rooster later, right? It didn't quite work out that way. The pecking order had already been firmly established among this Bad Chick Club.

However, I didn't realize what was going on. From the teenage area, I had this rooster who was just too handsome to go to the chopping block. *Perfect,* I thought, *I'll let him be the male leader of these Barred Rock Hens.* So, after chores, I grabbed him up from the teenage area and cuddled him, as I walked over to his new hens.

Seriously, I thought this was a rooster's dream... a new flock of ladies who had never been with a rooster. It was not all it was cackled out to be. I seriously thought that a big, tough rooster could hold his own, so I gently tossed him into the run without any reservations. Apparently, reservations *are* required in a new coop area.

---

[10] The social structure of chickens that defines who's in charge. Low-status chickens will literally be pecked when trying to assert dominance outside their rank.

The ladies, and I use that term loosely at this point, gathered around him like a biker gang gathers around someone who has just entered the wrong neighborhood. A few initial pecks were given, as the rooster looked around and turned in a circle trying to get a grasp on the situation. The Bad Chick Club was letting him know in no uncertain terms who was boss, and it wasn't him.

By evening chore time, I could see that he was being bullied to no end, and the ladies weren't letting up either. At this point, I just broke down and went into the run to rescue him. He was glad to be gathered up in my arms and taken out. This poor emasculated rooster was never brave again after this incident. Seriously, I never even saw him attempt to mount a female.

He had been clearly taught a lesson so great that he never regained his roosterly confidence. I ended up having to separate him for his own safety. While he looked like a magnificent rooster, he was just too much of a gentle giant, and we most certainly couldn't have that. His job was to protect the ladies, not run from them. Sadly, his fate ended up being the stew pot, though he was delicious.

So, what's a new owner to do that wants to add new chickens to their mature flock? Well, the best course of action is to introduce the newbies *after* dark. Not when it is starting to get dark. Not at dusk. But when it is fully dark outside. At that point, open up the door to the coop and quietly place the newbies one by one on the perch inside the coop. Because it is dark, the original chickens aren't going to stir during the night.

This allows them the full night to "sleep" with each other and become familiar with the newbies. The next morning, open the coop as normal, and your original chickens will come bustling out as is typical, while the newbies will most likely remain on their perches for a while as they become familiar with their new accommodations. This is perfectly normal and to be expected.

By noon, you should see that they are exploring their new home, and you might even catch them poking their head out the door with some curiosity. Just make sure there is food and water inside the coop as well as outside, so they have some options. If you have a particularly brave young chicken, she might venture out into the chicken run. And sometimes, you might have to rescue her at this point.

But by the second day, the pecking order should be firmly established, and the newbies will realize that they are second fiddle to the original chickens and any attempts at dominance will be thwarted. Many of my customers have heeded this advice, and all have exclaimed that it worked like a charm.

Another time, I dropped off new hens to brand new chicken owners. When you don't have an existing flock, then the rules are slightly different. You need to "marry" these new chickens to their new home. The best way to do this is to place them inside the coop together with food and water. Time of day doesn't matter, since there are no existing chickens. The important part here is to keep them in the coop for two full days.

So, what happens if you don't? Well, one customer found out the hard way. She placed all her new feathered friends into their run, and she assumed that they would just go into the coop that night (which they had never been in before). They didn't. And she spent some time chasing them down that evening and catching them one by one. It is important to establish where "home base" is for your chickens, and the only way to do that is to keep them inside for that length of time.

But as we showed earlier, if you have existing chickens, they will show any newbies the way home. But most of the time, the newbies will stay in the coop while the original chickens leave for the day, as their current location feels safer than out in the yard with the strange chickens.

And if you must integrate ducks (highly not recommended), then, just re-read the story about ducks over and over again from Chapter 3 until you convince yourself it is a bad idea. Just a word to the wise, stick with chickens or even add guinea fowl (if you need something loud and annoying to bother your neighbors), but don't add ducks.

Remember, if integration doesn't work correctly, then you most likely will have to resort to Chicken Jail, which we'll discuss later.

LESSONS LEARNED:

- Once the pecking order is firmly established, it is important to integrate chickens correctly to prevent them from being bullied, or worse, pecked to death.

- With an existing flock, it is best to put the newbies in *after* dark, so they can spend the night together and become familiar with each other.

- With a new flock, it is best to "marry" them to the new coop (ie. home base). Leave them in the coop for two full days with food and water before letting them outside.

Chapter 6

CHICK OR TREAT

f you thought the worst part was over, integrating the family dog is going to prove to be more challenging and time consuming, as they see chickens as tasty treats.

Farm Dog wasn't always 90 pounds. No, he started off at 25 pounds as an older puppy that had been returned to the shelter. The first few days I fostered him, he was super cuddly and wanted to sleep on my lap. When he was active, his favorite game was a simple, harmless little game called tug-o-war. Soon, I realized why he had been returned to the shelter.

He loved, and I mean *loved*, this game of tug-o-war, and he fought with a determination to win no matter what. And oh, he had a strong grip, which occasionally missed the rope. For good measure, he even added in sound effects of a big dog growling ferociously to make it all the more scary and intimidating. And of course, he ran around what would soon become our farm at warp puppy speed.

As we discussed in Chapter 1, when the first four baby chicks were hatched, he was super curious and calm. He sniffed them while I held them tightly in my hands. Later, they were moved to the porch, and he laid at full attention with his paws crossed watching them intently as they played inside their area.

It was a match made in heaven... or so we thought. As they got older and started to spread their wings a little, it was time to move them outside to a real coop and run. Farm Dog still enjoyed watching them inside their run and all seemed well.

Until the day that testosterone started coursing through the veins of the roosters, and they started crowing. It was suddenly *game on*, and they would run back and forth on either side of the fence with Farm Dog barking and growling, as if he wanted to kill that rooster.

This wasn't good. And it most certainly didn't help matters when Fabio became brave enough to peck Farm Dog right on the nose through the fence. He just lost his puppy mind at that point and bit the fence for good measure.

At this time, I decided to add guinea fowl to the farm, because they were supposed to eat ticks. And man, we were having a huge tick problem on the property. We couldn't go outside without bringing some of these little guys back inside with us.

So, the guinea keets[11] were transported to the farm, and Farm Dog was again curious about these new babies. Shockingly, he seemed unphased by the new arrivals in the car, even though they were deafeningly loud.

As they grew, it was time to start training them to free-range, because after all, they were there for natural tick control. We started by letting them into the run (with a wire roof because guineas can fly), and training them to go back into their coop at night. All was going well.

The next step was to open the run door toward late afternoon. At first, they were extremely timid, but they finally became brave enough to cross the threshold of their run into the unknown. We started

_____

[11] This refers to baby guineas ranging from one day old to 12 weeks old, which is the most fragile part of their lives. Afterwards, they are quite hardy and can fend for themselves.

herding them around the property with long sticks (see the instructional video on our YouTube channel @HendricksFarmMcBeanGA).

Now, Farm Dog had trouble with this phase, so he just stayed in the house for a time-out break. And after a few weeks, the guineas seemed thoroughly trained and ready to free-range on their own.

One morning, the guineas were let out, and they were making happy noises of contentment, as they walked around together pecking at the grass and feasting on invisible insects. I decided that it was a beautiful morning to work in the garden, and I let Farm Dog out to bask in the sun while I worked.

Now, the guineas would occasionally and without notice start squawking up a storm and take off in flight. I can recall several times eating breakfast and staring out the window, when quite unexpectedly, a flock of guineas would fly by. And after seeing this a few times, Farm Dog was intrigued.

On this particular morning, Farm Dog got a wild hair up his butt and decided that he himself would try to make the guineas fly. So, as he was laying in the yard, distinguished with his legs crossed in front of him, he suddenly jumped up and gave chase to the flock of guineas.

Astonished by this sudden attack, they immediately took flight and perched up in the highest trees. I stopped what I was doing to reprimand the dog, who gave me a confused look as to what the problem was. Then, I looked up, up, up into the trees. How was I possibly going to get them down?

Alas, I wasn't. They would come down when they were ready, which would be when Farm Dog was no longer in sight. This went on for weeks on end, and Farm Dog was really enjoying himself. When he gave chase, the look of pure ecstatic puppy joy was clearly visible on his face.

As a Black Mouth Cur, this type of dog naturally has a high-prey instinct just like a Malinois. Seriously, Farm Dog was just pure muscle and strutted around like the Lion King of the Farm, where you could see every movement in his body.

Thus, as a last resort, I started the "correction" collar. Now, I know this is controversial, but when used correctly, it can be quite effective. I started with a tone collar in the house. When he heard *beep, beep*, he immediately came over for his treat.

Later, I wouldn't even need the collar to call him, though instead of saying "come", I was half-singing *"Beep, beep, beep, BEEEEEEEEEEEP!"* I'm sure the neighbors thought I was crazy doing this on my front porch, but that's what he responded to.

After some time, when I called him and he didn't respond, he got a little vibrate. This was usually enough to get his attention, so he would come running to the beeps. It was time to test him outside... with the guineas.

You already know how this story is going to go, don't you?

At first, Farm Dog was on his best manners, sitting at full attention beside where I stood. But soon the puppy urges overtook his little body, and as the guineas approached our position, he could not control himself a moment longer and gave chase.

I vibrated him with the remote and loudly screamed, "NOOOOOOOOOOOOOOO!" He didn't change his course. The guineas were now in flight and headed right toward me. It was too late. One guinea hit me mid-flight in its attempt to escape. I was upset to say the least.

Farm Dog got a little shock. No response. A bigger shock. Nothing. Was this thing even on? But as we will learn in a later chapter, once dogs get into this zone, it is super difficult—if not impossible—to get them out of it.

It took weeks of never leaving him unsupervised with the guineas, which was quite annoying during gardening season. He learned to behave while I was watching, but occasionally the urge would overtake him again. Honestly, it took almost six months to train him, and he eventually caught one guinea. She died a few hours later from sheer fright at having been in his mouth, even though she appeared unhurt otherwise.

Today, he accepts them as part of the farm and just walks right by them like they don't even exist. After learning to accept the guineas, he was much more accepting when we added pigs and goats later.

Even though it feels like a dog will never learn to accept your feathered friends, they will *if* given enough time and training. Don't give up, which is easier said than done. If my stubborn Farm Dog can be trained, then I imagine any dog can be trained.

LESSONS LEARNED:

- Even though a dog may be fine with baby chicks, the dog's attitude may change when roosters start crowing or guineas start flying.

- It's best to train chickens and guineas to free-range *first* before bringing a dog into the equation, so only one variable is dealt with at a time.

- For high-prey dogs, a correction collar may be necessary. Always start the training without fowl being present, so the dog learns the collar meanings.

SECTION 3

You're a Chicken!

Chapter 7

SLIPPERY AS A SNAKE

SNAAAAAKE!

I do not like snakes. Period. And when I used to see a snake in the coop, well, I used to scream like a girl. Oh wait, I am a girl, so that is perfectly acceptable!

But at this point, I don't even scream anymore.

"Hey, Snake. What are you doing in here?"

Occasionally, I'll be going through chores in a half daze, since it becomes so routine after a while. I have reached in to grab eggs and not even noticed the snake until the last second. That's when I jump back, and I admit my heart goes to racing a little bit.

But at this point in my farming career, I have seen a lot of snakes in chicken coops *and* I have seen a lot of snakes eating eggs...

But I have seriously never, ever seen a snake do this.

Mr. Snake decided to be greedy on this particular day and eat one of Bertha's *egg*-normous Texas sized eggs. And Bertha lays some huge eggs that are so large that egg cartons just won't close around them.

To give you some reference, a small egg ranges from 1.5 to 1.75 ounces, a medium egg from 1.75 to 2.0 ounces, a large egg from 2.0 to 2.25 ounces, an XLarge egg from 2.25 to 2.50 ounces, and a Jumbo from 2.50 ounces upward.

Bertha's eggs averaged around 3.75 ounces. That's probably why she was such a very mean chicken, as that had to hurt to push out.

Unfortunately for Mr. Snake, things didn't go as planned for him, because I came upon him with an egg stuck in his throat. He had attempted to swallow one of Big Bad Bertha's Texas sized eggs, and he was having some difficulty with the size.

But when I opened up the coop, he decided to get the hell out of Dodge quickly when he saw me. And he bolted out of the nesting box and into the middle of the coop. So I started gathering eggs and minding my own business, and I didn't think much else of it.

Now, I probably should have killed that snake, since I knew without a shadow of a doubt that he would be back. But I didn't have a 22[12] handy on me, and I thought that a 9 millimeter hollow point might be a tad overkill (literally) for such a small creature. Plus, if I hit that egg in this throat, that would have exploded into a huge mess. It just wasn't worth it.

Suddenly, the sounds of someone choking in distress reached my ears. The labored gasps seemed to call for help. I looked around, and saw nothing but the snake. I was baffled, because those sounds couldn't possibly be coming from that snake.

Snakes were quiet, right?

As it turns out, Mr. Snake had really bitten off more than he could chew... literally. He was still trying to swallow that egg all the way down, but it was stuck and stuck good in his throat. That's when the horrible noises got louder. I mean, at first, I thought maybe he just had gas, right? *No!*

Mr. Snake was throwing up the egg! Literally, yellow puke came out of his mouth with the egg. You should have seen my face! *What the heck!*

---

[12] A good starter gun for training, as it fires small bullets and has little kickback. It's effective at killing small predators like snakes.

I didn't want to touch that egg, and it was definitely not going to be for sale. *Disgusting.* And at this point, it really took a lot to disgust me. Now, while most of these egg thieves are non-venomous, there are some, like rattlesnakes, that are venomous. If you can't tell, always err on the side of caution.

As a side note, there was one such venomous snake on my grandparents' farm. Why my granddad didn't kill it is beyond me. My grandparents had hundreds of chickens that free-ranged around the farm house and a giant chicken barn. I never really thought much of it at the time, though now I wish that I had asked a lot more questions.

My grandparents told us every single summer that there was a huge snake on the property. And on occasion, we might see it slithering here or there. It was thicker around than a man's fist and about as long as a person is tall. This thing was not to be messed with that was for sure.

What we didn't know was that it liked to go inside the horse's water trough.

One summer afternoon, my younger brother and I were playing out there, and the horses were coming in to get a drink. My younger brother, Jeffrey, always seemed to be doing something to put his life in danger, and today was no different. It truly is amazing that he made it to adulthood.

On this particular afternoon, Jeffrey climbed up on the side of the horse's water trough to look in, but the water was too dark to see what was at the bottom. As he was leaning over, he toppled head first into the trough. And that's when I saw a quick movement in the water. *Oh my goodness*! The snake was in there. I screamed bloody murder, because I feared that my little brother was about to die.

My mom heard and ran over. Grandad, who was nearby, came lightning fast. He reached in and grabbed Jeffrey out by his collar, as the snake was starting to wrap around his body. In this case, the snake wasn't interested in biting him as much as squeezing the life out of him. But Grandad was quick, and the snake fell back into the water.

My mom was hysterical that her baby had almost died. And the long, long lecture started about how dangerous that snake was and how we should stay far away from it. Again, why didn't someone kill it and eliminate the danger was beyond me at this young age.

Though I did find out later that it also ate several chicken eggs per day. Which again begged the question of why it was allowed to terrorize the farm for years to come. But maybe Grandad was endeared to it like we are with Bertha the Very Mean Chicken at our own farm. Who knows?

There are a few things that you can do to help keep snakes out of your coop. First, use hardware cloth instead of chicken wire. Snakes can go right through the wide holes in chicken wire. Second, you can use herbs themselves within the nesting boxes or plant these herbs around the coop to deter snakes, such as peppermint, marigold, rosemary, etc. Third, put mulch around the plants, as snakes don't like to slitter on sharp objects.

Most importantly, you should remove the eggs promptly each day. And remember that once a snake finds a nesting box full of eggs, it will continue to return until you kill it. Having a sharp shovel or small 22 handy on the farm to protect your chickens is almost essential as a farmer.

LESSONS LEARNED:

- Snakes will eventually find your chicken eggs in the coop, and they will continue to come back for this easy meal until stopped.

- Most snakes found eating chicken eggs are non-venomous, though occasionally a poisonous rattlesnake will join the club. Always err on the side of caution.

- A 22 is a great choice for dealing with small predators like snakes, especially for those new to handling guns as there is little kickback.

Chapter 8

THE MASKED BANDIT

At approximately 11 minutes after midnight, almost down to the second (because isn't that when most criminals start on their nightly prowls?), after sleeping all through the day, they roll out of bed with a nice big stretch, a mischievous grin on their faces, and an evil twinkle in their eyes.

While all of us decent, hard-working citizens are sound asleep in our warm and cozy beds, these hoodlums are preparing for a night on the town, putting on their long, dark coats and gloves... and don't forget the face mask! You know the one!

The full head cap that covers their entire face except for the two small eye holes, and the small opening for the mouth. Yeah, that's the one! Can you tell how upset I am over these guys? So mad that I could spit nails.

But this time, the Masked Bandit was *caught on camera* prowling around our farm!

Being an opportunist, he snuck around with Ninja-like skills looking for what he could steal!

Horrified, I watched it all play out on camera, as he looked for weaknesses in our security. Standing up on tippy toes looking inside windows and shaking doorknobs hoping that they would pop open.

The suspect appeared to be overweight from one too many free dinners. A distinct tattoo was prominent on his rear end, which seems cool nowadays for these whippersnappers.

He could possibly be described as one big teddy bear, the kind that makes all the ladies swoon. But he also had a bad boy persona too, because what girl isn't drawn to that?

With his razor sharp teeth similar to a vampire's deadly fangs ready to sink into unsuspecting flesh, not to mention his long, witch-like nails similar to the meat-ripping claws of Freddy Krueger from *A Nightmare on Elm Street*, he viciously tore open a chicken tractor like it was made from paper and proceeded to violently rip the heads off six teenage chickens.

Don't worry! I won't show you those pictures! The crime scene was too gruesome. The blood splattered everywhere told the story of the horrific attack.

Racoons should be considered ARMED AND DANGEROUS! Even though they are cute and appear to be cuddly, do *not* approach them in real life. They can carry rabies in the worst case scenario. Best case scenario, you get an ass whooping, and they walk away unscathed.

Honestly, it is a never-ending game of cat and mouse with racoons, coyotes, hawks, etc. And once you increase your defenses in one area, they find a weakness in another. This is the life of a farmer! *Sigh*

It's a constant juggling act between taking care of animals and protecting them from other animals. Unfortunately, farming isn't as easy as Norman Rockwell painted it to be.

So, how do we protect our chickens from racoons?

Well, there are several things that can help. I prefer traps with canned tuna, peanut butter, or gooey marshmallows. Their favorite is honey buns[13]. Now, the tuna can packed in water (not oil)

---

[13] Their favorite honey bun is made by TasteKakes, which is covered in chocolate icing and is stuffed with cream filling at a whopping 580 calories.

sometimes has to sit outside in a trap for two weeks before it gets disgustingly smelly enough to entice a raccoon, so don't lose hope.

I'd been waiting for weeks—almost losing all hope, I might add—when suddenly those *beepity beep beep beeps* finally clucked up.

After those masked bandits broke into a chicken tractor that had been wrapped three times in fencing wire and violently ripped the heads off hundreds of chickens, I wasn't able to go to the butcher that month. And since this was the fourth time they had outsmarted me and still broke in despite all my attempts to reinforce my tractors, well, I was really upset.

Yep, for their night of fun, these guys had cost me thousands of dollars. This was an all-out *war* now!

I borrowed a couple traps from my friend and set them strategically around a chicken tractor with some sacrificial chickens inside the tractor. Next, I baited the traps with delicacies like canned tuna, fresh eggs, and peanut butter.

I checked the traps religiously every single morning.

The first morning, the peanut butter was gone, but the trap hadn't sprung. *Dang it!*

The next morning, the peanut butter was gone again, but the trap *had* sprung... with no critter inside.

Beepity beep beep beep!

If you haven't noticed yet, farming comes with lots of fowl language. This went on for over two weeks! And then, when I had almost given up, I saw what I had been waiting for...

Two racoons in the big trap with an empty can of tuna! A two for one special! Hot diggity dog!

They gave their most impressive "feel sorry for us" look, even putting their paws on the other in a protective manner, but they were goners. Two 22 bullets was all it took. Their death sentence was swift and merciful, unlike the deaths of the hundreds of chickens they had caused.

If I had more time that day, I would have skinned them to make two Limited Edition Coonskin Hats. Yep, Davy Crockett style... King of the Wild Frontier. Someone told me that coons are good eating, like the dark meat of turkey. I passed.

Unfortunately, this victory was short lived. Once racoons find a good source of food, they send a telegram to all their relatives far and wide to invite them to this great feast... ie., your chickens.

And so it was in this case, as the war continues to this very day.

But I learned some lessons from this whole ordeal. First, chickens are defenseless and easy prey, so you must protect them. And racoons can rip through wood and wire, so they can pretty much get through anything, especially when motivated by scared chickens.

Second, Animal Control will *not* relocate racoons due to the possible rabies. Therefore, if you don't dispatch them yourself, they will euthanize them. To relocate them is cruel, since they are highly territorial (and so are the animals where they may be dropped off), so you aren't doing them any favors with relocation.

Lastly, you can never make a coop or tractor too secure. Consider electrical wire to light those guys up or even safety latches[14] that confuse most adults too.

Seriously, double-check your coop to find any weaknesses. Ask a buddy or child to get in who knows nothing about your coop. If they can't do it, then you at least stand a chance of outsmarting a racoon.

---

[14] This adds extra security to a standard latch by requiring the user to pull back and compress a spring to open the door.

LESSONS LEARNED:

- Raccoons may appear cute and cuddly, but they should be considered ARMED AND DANGEROUS. Do not attempt to relocate, as they are highly territorial.

- Raccoons can rip through wood and wire, so continuous reinforcement of chicken coops is necessary. Or consider hot wire to light those guys up.

- Raccoons love sweets, especially anything chocolate that has cream filling. However, they can also be baited with gooey marshmallows, canned tuna, fresh eggs, and peanut butter.

Chapter 9

BEING IN THE DOGHOUSE

When you think of predators, you probably picture racoons or even foxes... but dogs? Probably not, right? I felt the same way at one time.

December 4, 2021 was a cold and overcast day. The kind of day, where you just want to curl up in bed under a nice, warm blanket. I remember it well. The air was chilly, and I had been cold all day long, when the sun finally started playing peek-a-poo through the clouds in the late afternoon. A little before four in the afternoon, I heard a loud commotion outside. Thinking that it was coyotes that were hungry, I grabbed my shotgun by the door and headed out on a brisk walk, having decided to investigate quickly before starting evening chores. I would never have guessed what was waiting for me out in the chicken yard on that fateful day that changed my life forever.

As I approached the gate leading to the chicken yard, I didn't quite comprehend what I saw covering the ground. I just saw a streak of red... blood. And then I gasped in horror, as I realized that there were chicken body parts scattered everywhere. It was like I was just seeing everything in slow motion like it was a horror movie. This just couldn't be happening. It didn't even seem real. I went completely on auto-pilot.

I approached the main enclosure, where there were more torn-apart chicken bodies. Some were still alive gasping for air. And then, I looked up and my eyes locked with the eyes of not one, but two pitbulls. One of the two still had a chicken in his mouth with blood dripping down his chin. When he saw me, he dropped the bloody chicken from his mouth, and his eyes locked directly on me. He was blood-thirsty and in kill-mode, and he had just seen his next target... *me*!

At that point, the dogs split to circle me... the prey. Thankfully, I had lots of gun training under my belt, being a Native Texan and all. And I was quick on the draw, and the shotgun was up on my shoulder in a split second. I fired on the first dog, turned to the second dog, and took another shot, and then back to the first. Though the shots were hitting center mass, they did nothing to phase the dogs, except to make them angrier. I unloaded the entire shotgun and then threw it to the ground.

I don't even remember drawing my sidearm or taking off the safety, but it was suddenly in front of my body firing hollow-point bullets into these dogs. First, right, then left, then right, as the dogs continued to come at me from opposite directions, then back to left until the magazine was empty. At that point, they had finally dropped to the ground despite the adrenaline coursing through their veins.

But even so, as the one was bleeding out, he was still trying to crawl toward me. It was terrifying, to say the least. At that moment, I realized the severity of the situation, as I looked around at the bloody mess of dogs and chickens. It felt surreal, and I started shaking. Then, I started crying, as I saw the pain and agony of those mauled chickens, which lay there slowly dying. There was nothing I could do to help them survive.

The police were called, and my neighbor came over as well. We gathered up chickens, while they were passing away in our arms. Hundreds of chickens were dismembered and scattered through the hatchery and woods. The dogs had torn through fences and bitten their way through wood coops. There had been no stopping them. They had gone through three perimeter fences to reach the hatchery in the middle of the acreage.

One of the only roosters to survive was Dwayne the Barred Rock. He was a tough old bird. He even had teeth marks in his back from the dogs, where they had grabbed hold of him at one point. But this giant boy wasn't about to let them win. I'm not even sure how he survived the whole ordeal, but he was later found in the woods a good distance away from his assigned run.

But this nightmare was far from over. You see, the owner of these dogs was responsible. We posted on Facebook that two pitbulls were found and could be picked up at the animal shelter. I failed to mention that they went out in body bags. The next day, I filled two large city trash cans with chicken body parts, as I bawled my eyes out until I was worn out with grief. My life had changed, and I would never be the same after that.

The owner did eventually claim his dogs at the animal shelter and was charged, but not before threatening to burn down the animal shelter and kill the person who killed his dogs. Social media went crazy, as people threatened me and called me a "dog killer". But the truth is that I was in fear for my life when those pitbulls charged me, as they would have ripped me apart just like those chickens.

And while I know that pitbulls have a bad rap, and this story doesn't help their case, I firmly believe that it doesn't matter what breed of dog you have, the owner is responsible for training that dog. Any dog can be good or bad regardless of the breed. Unfortunately, these pitbulls were not trained well, as this was the sixth time there had been a report filed against the owner, with one of those being a prior case of killing chickens.

In hindsight, hot wire[15] might have helped protect my chickens, but those dogs were so determined that I'm not sure that would have even stopped them. The moral of this story is that you can never be too cautious about protecting your chickens. They are easy prey.

Luckily, our farm kept going despite this tragedy, though many told me they would have just closed up shop and given up on their dream. Not me! I went to court and testified, and the owner was found guilty.

---

[15] This is the farm term for electrical wire run around the perimeter of a fence to either keep animals in or keep predators out.

LESSONS LEARNED:

- Neighboring dogs might attack your chickens, so fencing should not only keep your chickens in but help deter dogs from coming in as well.

- When a dog is in kill mode with adrenaline coursing through his veins, it can take a lot to stop him. The owner is responsible for any damage their dog does to your chickens.

- It is best to always carry a firearm on your body, as it is better to have it and not need it than to need it and not have it.

SECTION 4

Handling Cocks

Chapter 10

THE TAMING OF THE COCK

Every chicken owner has a horror story about that one rooster. I have one too! No, worse than a story, I have a video of me being attacked by a rooster. You can see it for yourself on YouTube[16].

So embarrassing! And if it hadn't been for the tree behind me, I would have fallen backward from that rooster attack. Every single morning that I open up the chicken coops, I know exactly what is about to happen. It doesn't matter what rooster it is, they are all going to do the same thing.

---

[16] The YouTube channel is @HendricksFarmMcBeanGA along with Facebook and Instagram.

Honestly, I'm not sure if they all go to the same rooster-training school or what, but every morning, those roosters are waiting intently... to jump out of that coop. Sometimes, they're on the floor, while other times up on the perch. It's more impressive when they are up on the perch, because when they jump down to the ground, there is a gigantic thud as they hit the ground with all their might. I swear the ground shakes, or it could just be me who is shaking.

Mind you, all this happens within seconds, before they initiate their aggressive charge. You seriously haven't lived (or appreciated life for that matter) until a rooster has chased you down to do physical bodily harm to you. And I have heard some tell me how gentle and loving their rooster is... until it hits puberty.

Then, all bets are off.

One of our farm family members, who we'll call Mrs. D., said the same thing about how precious her Polish rooster, Ringo, was until that fateful day when hormones started pulsating through his little body. He suddenly realized he was a rooster with a crazy badass hairstyle and started enjoying a reign of terror that reached a whole new level. Mrs. D. actually texted me that she was terrified of him and afraid to go outside to feed her chickens. Sensing her fear, he became bolder! He would chase her down every single time he saw her.

Mrs. D. would pull back the curtain just a smidge and peer out her living room window. There he was... waiting. The moment she would try to leave her house, he would pursue her. All she wanted to do was make it to her car, but alas, there was Ringo... staring at the front door. She knew what would happen. Her screams of pure fright could be heard ringing through the entire neighborhood, as she tried to escape this dreadful creature whom she had once loved so dearly.

While you might be laughing and thinking that I can't possibly be serious, let me assure you that I'm totally serious. Rooster attacks can be quite serious. And around the six month mark, testosterone starts pumping through a rooster's veins, and he suddenly thinks that he can take on the world. This is great if you have a predator trying to attack your laying hens. This is bad if he is coming after you.

I believe that President Theodore Roosevelt gave the best rooster advice when he said, "Speak softly and carry a *big stick*." And yes, this does work! Of course, I use a one inch PVC pipe, but it's the same principle. No, we aren't going to use the stick to beat the rooster, though I'm sure that it has crossed the minds of some chicken owners.

Most of the time, you just need to give the rooster a little poke in his direction for him to clear his head. Sometimes it takes multiple jabs in the rooster's direction for him to get the memo. But these defensive measures along with the stick allowing you to keep him at a distance does eventually train him that you're not to be reckoned with and that you rule this roost (not him!).

So, what happened when Mrs. D. implemented the stick method? She texted back, *"Well, I am once again Queen of the Farm! With broom in hand, all roosters (namely Ringo) run in terror and bow before me. I only had to brandish said implement once and the effect was complete surrender. Thank you for the sage advice."*

But before you start thinking that all roosters are evil, you do occasionally get a nicer one, or one that can be tamed with chicken cuddles[17]. On our very first hatch out that we discussed in Chapter 1, we ended up with two roosters. We eventually named one Fabio, because he was quite a ladies' man, and the other one, we named Delicious, because he just could not behave. He lived up to his name at the dinner table a few months later.

Now, Fabio wasn't always gentle. In fact, I was terrified of him at first. But eventually, it was

---

[17] Many chickens like to be held and even petted. Don't be surprised to hear cooing and other soft noises similar to a cat when they are enjoying the attention.

discovered that Fabio would calm immediately when picked up and cuddled. It was crazy, because the way he held his head so high when picked up, it was like he was telling the ladies that this was how Kingly roosters were supposed to be treated.

Other roosters didn't succumb to the chicken cuddles like Fabio. In which case, they had to be grabbed up and hung by their legs upside down in complete and utter humiliation. Doing this every day for about a week broke the rooster's desire to attack, because he knew he would be embarrassed as he hung upside down. Afterwards, it was like he had lost some of his mojo in front of the ladies.

The last way is to "mount" him like he does to the hens, which is his way of establishing dominance with his harem of girls. You push the rooster completely to the ground with the palm of your hand, where his chest is touching the ground. Then, the palm of your right hand holds his backend down, similar to where his feet would be when standing on a hen. With your left hand, make a V shape with your first two fingers and put the rooster's neck in the middle. Using this V, push his head down to the ground, like how he would grab on to a hen's head and push her head to the ground. Hold him there for a minute and then let him back up. This doesn't hurt the rooster in the least, at least physically, but it will damage his ego.

Now that you know some ways to tame a rooster (stick, cuddles, hanging, or mounting), you need to be aware of the four ways that a rooster can attack you, and sometimes they use multiple methods in one attack.

In the example above, Mrs. D.'s Ringo loved chasing as his preferred method. Obviously, this is just a precursor to one of the next three attack methods, since this is more than a game to him. The goal is to catch you and flog you with his wings to get you disoriented while using his spurs to stab you before finally pecking you to your death. This is why it is extremely unwise to leave small children out unsupervised with farm animals.

Fabio loved pecking. And while it may appear cute when they are young. You definitely want to stop this behavior before it becomes a full-fledged weapon that can leave you bloody (or worse, dead if they hit a vein).

And our Black Copper Marans loved spurring, where they jump up and try to inflict damage on you using their back spurs. Like a cowboy with boot spurs, these sharp bony protrusions on the backside of their bottom legs can actually inflict deep puncture wounds and leave you with a trip to the emergency room for stitches.

But the really special roosters love flogging, where they jump up and flap you with their wings.

There's added bonus points if they flog your face. This doesn't sound like it could hurt from such a tiny, lightweight bird. But for those of us that have experienced it, you already know that this hurts and can leave your skin beet red.

Remember, you have to take charge. The earlier, the better. Roosters must learn that you rule the roost, not them. Start holding roosters while they are young and stop seemingly innocent behavior like pecking early on. If needed, you can hang baby chicks upside down by their legs without any physical harm.

LESSONS LEARNED:

- While chicken cuddles work on some roosters like Fabio, other roosters like Ringo require being jabbed with a stick to learn boundaries.

- Other methods to tame a rooster are to physically hold him down in a "mount" position or to hang him upside down. Both of these will embarrass the rooster in front of the ladies.

- Roosters may chase, peck, spur, or flog you. If they're particularly feisty, they may even use all four on you within one planned attack. Stop this behavior early while they are young chicks.

Chapter 11

STOP CLUCKIN' AROUND

Just like an older sibling that picks on you relentlessly, some of these chickens (both roosters and hens) will sometimes just get out of control. They will tear feathers out of other hens and chase them around. Other times, it becomes more severe, as these bullies will guard food sources and prevent them from eating and cause them to lose a lot of weight. And roosters add to all this trauma by literally "raping" hens to death at times. This is why it's important to take the time to watch your chickens and see what is going on.

Now, I will state for the record that even though roosters have a full harem of beautiful concubines, they always have that one hen who is their favorite. Gloria was this favorite hen. She was a beautiful Buff Orpington hen with blond feathers that made the sun jealous. And the word beautiful doesn't do her justice. Let's just say that she was drop dead gorgeous as far as hens go. She was the kind that might even rival the beauty of Princess Kate herself in the chicken world of course.

I mean, all the boys liked Gloria, a little too much if you ask me. So, when I was out gathering eggs one evening, imagine my surprise when I opened up the back coop door to find Gloria wedged between two boards of the pallet walls. Yeah, we're rednecks down here in the South, and we build our coops out of used pallets. Remember when I stated in Chapter 4 that chickens actually preferred Section 8 to more lavish housing?

Gloria had been viciously attacked by a gang of roosters, as they had taken turns mounting her. The evidence was a trail of her beautiful blonde feathers scattered in a path leading to her hiding spot. Just like baby chicks play dead to avoid predators, hens also have a similar modus operandi. Similiar to puppies who believe that if they can't see you, then you can't see them either, hens will do their best to hide openly from roosters. Unfortunately, this can sometimes lead to crazy predicaments like the one that Gloria found herself in.

I tried to help Gloria, but she was stuck real good. And for the life of me, I couldn't figure out how she got herself in this mess. I mean, she obviously squeezed into this little nook, but she couldn't get out. Her eyes were even starting to glaze over a bit, as she had given up all hope on life. She. Just. Couldn't. Go. On.

Okay, maybe that was a little over dramatic there, but she literally looked like she was ready to die right there. Chickens do that. Even baby chicks that fall over will start to die on you. But as soon as you put them back up on their feet, they're like, "Oh, I'm fine," and they run off to play again.

Time and time again, I've seen this strange behavior to lose all hope of survival.

After trying frantically to free her for a good ten minutes by wiggling her backward and then forward—I mean, she got herself in there somehow—she was not budging one little centimeter. It was ridiculous. And since she was seriously giving up all hope of life itself, I decided that it was time for the Jaws of Life.

I hurried my buns over to the shed and retrieved a small crowbar and a hammer, so I could gently pry open the boards and make room for her to wiggle out. Well, when I reappeared with tools in hand, her eyes grew huge with fright, as if her day had just gotten a whole lot worse. I'm sure that she figured she was a goner now.

But with a few small whacks of the hammer against the small crowbar I had wedged in, the nails pried loose just enough to where Gloria was able to wiggle out. Oh, and she cackled up quite the storm, as she ran to tell the other ladies about her near death experience. You just can't imagine all the things that chickens do all day long.

Personally, I feel the majority of problems are caused by Bertha the Very Mean Chicken, who you will learn more about later. Knowing her antics, she probably double-dog-dared Gloria into this, but I can't prove a thing. Again, chickens will sometimes get themselves stuck somewhere as a means to avoid a bullying situation.

But seriously, when designing space considerations, it is important to note that you don't want more than one rooster to 10-12 hens, or the roosters will actually gang up on the hens and "gang rape"[18] them. I have seen it way too many times. These roosters can literally rape a hen to death over the course of just a few days. It is no joking matter here.

---

[18] This happens when there are too many roosters in your flock. When mounting a hen, their nails will rip, tear, and claw a hen's back causing sometimes severe injuries and possible infection. Eventually, the hen will withdraw from the flock to protect herself and may even stop laying eggs from the stress.

Just yesterday, I had a VIP customer stop by the farm with seven, count them, *seven* teenage roosters. Remember how we discussed the true meaning of "straight run" in Chapter 2? Well, she had purchased 16 baby chicks in the Spring. I had reiterated that they were straight-run, and she said that it was fine. Okay...

But as these cute babies grew up, they started to crow and the testosterone started to course through their veins. And seven roosters to nine hens is *not* a good ratio.

As you can imagine, these roosters started getting busy, and their first target was an unsuspecting Salmon Faverolles, which is quite small and dainty. Within days, all her neck feathers were gone, and she was hiding in the corner. So, her owner tried to find a home for all these roosters, but as we all know, nobody wants extra roosters. She was visibly upset, as she loved them and they were indeed beautiful specimens.

But, as you already know from Chapter 2, usually 50% of all straight-run chicks become roosters. In the olden days, this was great, as half the chicks became egg layers and half became a Sunday dinner. But today, most people buying chicks don't have the heart to dispatch their own chickens, as they grow very attached to them. And this lady was no different. She had even played their favorite classical music for them on the drive over to our farm.

In a later chapter, we'll go into more detail about how to deal with bully hens in a flock. And while you can buy aprons for the backs of hens to help protect them from the roosters, there really is only one solution for too many roosters... Freezer Camp, which we will discuss in the next chapter.

LESSONS LEARNED:

- It's important to keep the rooster to hen ratio at one rooster to 10-12 hens in order to prevent "gang rape" of just one hen.

- When being bullied, a chicken may "hide" in plain sight. In addition to physical injuries, the stress of the event can also cause them to stop laying eggs and/or stop eating food.

- It's not uncommon for both baby chicks and adult chickens to start giving up their will to live when they feel that their current situation is beyond fixing.

Chapter 12

A TRIP TO FREEZER CAMP

This is the thing nobody really wants to talk about, and many new chicken owners will blatantly tell me that they could *never* dispatch a chicken themselves (ie. kill them), especially after raising them from baby chicks.

So let's say that you played some Chicken Roulette and bought straight-run chicks like I discussed in Chapter 2, and now you don't know what to do with the extra roosters. Sounds about right.

I won't beat around the bush here. This is the hard part. I really do understand.

On our first batch of chickens from Chapter 1, you will remember that we had four beautiful precious chicks hatch out. One was clearly a rooster, as he was constantly charging our hand. Then, a second one became obvious a few months later. But we were like most new owners, "It will be fine." But at the six month mark, it was clear that it was anything but fine.

Those two hens were no match for the two roosters. Let's just be bluntly honest here, so you might want to brace yourself. Even though roosters don't have a penis (seriously!), they can still "rape" a hen to death. And multiple roosters in a pen will "gang rape" a hen to death. I have literally seen this with my own eyes. A rooster will mount a hen and then quickly hop off while another rooster immediately hops on.

Over the course of several days, those roosters will pull out the neck and back feathers of the hens. Then, they will start digging into their exposed bare skin with their sharp toenails. Of course, at this point, the hens will start hiding like Gloria did in the last chapter. Eventually, they will be too scared to go get food and water, and their health will start going downhill fast. Sometimes, these back wounds will even get infected.

This is why it is so vitally important that you have only one rooster to about 10 to 12 hens. This will ensure that all the eggs are fertilized, so you can hatch more chicks (and yes, you can eat fertilized eggs too). Now, you can obviously have more hens to one rooster, but it isn't advisable to have less than 10 to 12 hens to any rooster. Some of the smaller ones, like the Polish breed, (Ringo from Chapter 10) have been known to be more aggressive (talk about little man syndrome!).

Remember Fabio and his brother, who was named Delicious? These teenagers were aggressive. But when push came to shove, Fabio was the gentler of the two, so Delicious got grabbed up to head to the chopping block. He was cooked up, and boy oh boy he sure did live up to his name. A real chicken has so much flavor compared to grocery store chickens, but most people have never experienced this for themselves.

One thing to keep in mind is that it is really difficult to "rehome" roosters. Yes, there are some people who are in need of a rooster, but those people are few and far between. Most of the time, a rooster will be headed to his fate of the dinner plate. On the other hand, there are some people who are eager to take roosters for "cockfighting[19]", which is illegal. But nonetheless, you have to be careful about who you give your rooster to, so be sure to ask plenty of questions.

My question to people is, "If you already put all the time and money into this rooster to get him to full-size, why would you give him away instead of having this healthy meat for yourself?" Even hens that are slowing down their laying around the two year mark make a wonderful "stewing bird" with the richest broth that you have ever had in your life. Be sure to add a tablespoon of apple cider vinegar to the crockpot, as it helps to pull all the nutrients from the bones while it simmers on low for 24 to 48 hours.

But before you dispatch your chickens, it's easier if you separate them and provide just water for 24 hours before (no food), so that their crop and intestines empty out. This just makes for a cleaner process. But it isn't the end of the world if you just grab a rooster that needs to go who still has a full crop (look at their neck).

As a word of caution, be sure to correctly slice their neck, so the animal doesn't suffer. A few years ago, a guy decided to hang the roosters upside down

---

[19] Even though cockfighting is illegal in the United States, people will still buy "extra" unwanted roosters to participate in this bloody and inhumane event, where two roosters literally fight to the death.

(which is my preferred method) and slice their neck, so they bleed out quickly. This is actually pretty humane and more kosher. Unfortunately, he didn't listen to the fact that your knife needs to be really sharp, and I mean sharp. He sliced the neck, and blood started coming out. The bird flopped around, and then closed its eyes and hung still.

After a few minutes, the next step is to scald the bird in very hot water. So, the bird was taken down and carried over to the scalding water. Right before its head touched the hot water, its eyes popped open, and it jerked away from the hot water. I was shocked and so upset with the guy. He hadn't killed the bird, and I was horrified that it had suffered. I insisted that he take the bird back to the gallows and slice the neck to put the bird out of its suffering. Talk about being upset. I was that day!

Thus, always ensure that you use a sharp knife. Do *not* use a dull knife. Personally, I find it easier to use my left hand to hold and pull the head down when it is hanging by its feet, and to use my right hand with the knife to quickly slice the vein in the side of the neck. Then, jump back, because the bird will start flapping around and blood will shoot out. When we teach butchering classes, I tell everyone, this is the *last* step in the process when you are learning.

It is best to start by observing the first time, then maybe just bag the finished bird next. Then, maybe operate the plucker when you're ready or dip the bird in scalding water. At that point, you should be ready to clean the inside of the bird. And let's be honest, some people never have the heart to kill the bird but can do everything else. And if you feel that's you, that's okay too.

The important part is to honor the animal's life and not waste any of it. I think too often we take for granted where our food comes from and how much work goes into it. The grocery store shelves are crammed packed with all kinds of meat, and there's a lot of waste. Homesteaders[20] have a greater appreciation for their food, and I think that is a good thing. This is especially true if you have a very mean chicken like Bertha in the next chapter.

---

[20] This type of person loves being self-sufficient and living off the land. They will usually have chickens at a minimum and a vegetable garden, though some also milk goats and keep pigs.

LESSONS LEARNED:

- One rooster should have 10 to 12 hens in the flock. Any extra roosters should be butchered by the six month mark, before they become aggressive with the hens.

- It's important to have a sharp knife when dispatching chickens to ensure they do not suffer. Verify they are dead before dunking them in scalding water.

- When learning to butcher chickens, it's best to work with an experienced homesteader, so you can observe the entire process the first time.

SECTION 5

Chicks with Attitude

MUGSHOT 335852

Chapter 13

SHE'LL PECK YOUR EYE OUT!

ertha... If that name doesn't strike fear in your heart...

Well, let me tell you, it should. It certainly does mine.

Bertha the Very Mean Chicken, as she was fittingly named, is horribly mean. Where do I even begin?

Should I tell you how she likes to peck all the eggs in her nesting box out of pure spite, so I can't sell them?

Or how she tried to peck me in the wrist, so I'd bleed out to death? I know, I know, you think I'm exaggerating, but I'm not. Perhaps you'll believe me when you see her mugshot for the time she was charged with attempted murder.

Oh, what about how she has tried to form a coup and overthrow the farm multiple times?

Go ahead, and take your pick. Bertha is just pure evil. And why she hasn't ended up in the stewpot yet is only because of her raving email fans. Which by the way, shame on *you* for encouraging her bad behavior.

So, let's start with how she likes to peck all the eggs in her nesting box out of pure spite. Now, chickens don't always lay an egg every day. Their cycle can be up to 26 hours, which means some days are skipped. And multiple hens will share the same nesting box in one day. Let's do some Chicken Math together!

There are 365 days in a year. We all agree on that, right? Depending on the breed, some chickens only lay 200 eggs per year, others 250, and others 300, and occasionally 350[21] if you are really lucky!

Bertha is at a *negative* 1,273 for the year, because she happily (perhaps gleefully) destroys the eggs of the other chickens in her nesting box. Why are you laughing? Again, please stop encouraging her behavior!

---

[21] Commercial hybrid breeds are known to lay 350 eggs in their first year, declining in their second year. Most homestead heritage breeds like Rhode Island Reds average 250 eggs per year.

Back to the point, chickens naturally slow down in egg production during the cold and dark winter months. But they also slow down during the heat of summer. So, it can be extremely difficult to fulfill orders when the hens go on strike during the Winter and Summer *or* when Bertha is pecking everything in sight.

You're probably wondering why I don't stop her from pecking the eggs. Well, if only it were so easy. Let's just start with the time that she nearly killed me. Didn't you know that a chicken can actually kill you by pecking the vein in your wrist?

I mean, your chances of being killed by a chicken are actually low, but don't get me wrong, it's *never zero*. And with Bertha, your chances of being killed are much higher.

You see, Bertha aims for this vein. She ain't messing around. When she determines that she is about to be evicted from her nest and she has missed your vein, she will then peck her egg *and* every other egg in the nest. Seriously, I'm losing half a dozen XLarge eggs per day with this Crazy Chick.

Then, she leaves the nest in a huff, squawking up a storm like a Karen in a crowded department store, while all the other ladies gather around to find out why she was triggered this time. Let me tell you...it's annoying at best.

So when someone asks me, *"Why are your eggs sooooo expensive?"* I just stare at them and blink before taking in a deep breath and answering, *"Do you want to go gather eggs from Bertha yourself?"* How much is your life worth to you? Seriously, Every. Single. Day. That I have to deal with Bertha, I see my whole life flash before my eyes.

But chickens are smart, and Bertha is smarter than the average chicken. Unfortunately, this time, she got herself arrested for attempted murder and got her mugshot published in our weekly newsletter. *"How?"* you might ask. By aiming at the vein in my wrist again. Shouldn't I have known to expect this behavior?

Well, this time she had a new trick up her sleeve, and she almost got me. Instead of just doing her normal single peck, she had been practicing a double peck, so I wouldn't be expecting the second one. What a *beepity beep beep beep*! At this point, I am thinking about making chicken for Saturday's lunch.

So, by popular demand—*Drum roll please or just cluck in unison*—take a good, hard look at Bertha's mugshot.

Seriously, would you mess with that face? That's what I thought. Definitely a negative!

And yet, I risk my life. Every. Single. Day. Dealing with this *beepity beep beep beep.*

Now, my Grandma warned me about the likes of Bertha when I was still young and visiting her farm one summer. My grandparents' farm was a magical place, where we would spend a few weeks every summer. They had gone through the Great Depression, and nothing, and I mean nothing, was wasted.

Their house had can goods stashed here and there, under the stairs, down in the root cellar, and even out in the barn. You never knew when you would open a cabinet, and have one of those wobbly cans fall out and bonk you on the head.

And they had chickens... lots and lots of chickens. The chicken house was a long tunnel that seemed to go on forever. And the chickens free-ranged all over the place. Never did I imagine in a million years that I would grow up to be a Crazy Chicken Lady, but here I am living the dream.

One thing that I do remember was that my Grandma had an iron-clad glove that went all the way up to her elbow. She used it when she would steal eggs from under the broody hens[22]. Without it, she said that a chicken could peck you in the vein of your wrist and you would bleed out to death. I admit it, these stories were scary as a child.

---

[22] These hens are keeping their nest of eggs warm, so that they hopefully hatch at the end of 21 days. Between the raging hormones and maternal instinct, it can be nearly impossible to remove them from their nest without a huge fight.

And then one day... one of those chickens tried to kill my Grandma, using the very tactic she had described to us. I literally saw it with my own wide eyes! My Grandma survived, but I am pretty well convinced those chickens were the ancestors of Bertha the Very Mean Chicken.

I know, I know, after such a horror story, you're probably wondering if having chickens is such a good idea after all. But I never wear an iron-clad, full-arm glove when gathering eggs here at our farm, even with Bertha. And I do have a trick of my own that might make my Grandma proud.

You see, I take an old egg carton, and I close it around Bertha's head, so she can't peck me *(or try to kill me as the case may be)*. Don't worry, this doesn't hurt the chicken in the least... except maybe her pride. And then, while I'm holding the egg carton around her head...

And believe you me, at this point, she is turning her head and pecking both sides—violently, I might add—with all her chicken might.

While one hand is securely holding the egg carton over her head, my other hand carefully reaches underneath her, and I pick her up and gently toss her out. Oh, you thought I was just going to steal eggs and let her be. Oh, no! I toss Bertha out.

She isn't happy, of course. And she is quite vocal about the rude room service. But the whole moral of this story is to be careful around broody hens. Farming isn't all fun and games. I don't put on a beautiful, checkered sundress and skip out barefoot to the chicken coop with a woven straw basket. No.

I come prepared for war. And you should be on your guard too.

But there are other things that you should be on guard about too... like how to correctly play the game of *catch me if you can* like Estelle in the next chapter.

LESSONS LEARNED:

- Most heritage chicken breeds average 250 eggs per year, where the majority of eggs are laid in the Spring and Fall while Summer and Winter have the least amount laid.

- It's always important to be on your guard when trying to gather eggs from a nest with a broody hen, as she will try to peck you to protect her unborn chicks.

- If you don't have an iron-clad glove to protect yourself, the next best thing is an egg carton closed around the chicken's head while you gather eggs.

Chapter 14

CATCH ME IF YOU CAN!

L ong sigh* It seriously never ends around here. *Shaking my head in disbelief*

That particular morning, the weather was beautiful. Just the perfect temperature that was comfortable while still having a little chill in the air. Ahhh... it was such a nice break from the heat. But alas, Georgia weather can change in the blink of an eye. And by the afternoon, almost to the minute when I was about to start evening chores, it started pouring cats and dogs. So I sat on the porch with my farm dog and waited... and waited... and waited... and waited.

Finally, it slowed down a little, though it never completely stopped. I tended to the goats (who melt in the rain) and pigs (who relish a good mud bath), and mind you that at this point, it was just raining. No thunder. No lightning. Just rain. And suddenly out of nowhere, *BAM*!

Lightning hit something nearby, though I never discovered exactly what. It literally shook the ground, and I ducked for cover. At this point, I continued to the chicken yard, not knowing that the lightning strike was about to change the course of my afternoon. While attending to the chickens, something black caught my eye. It was small, quick, and definitely out of place. And then, I saw it again.

A Black Copper Marans[23] hen, and man, was she fast!

That lightning must have scared the life out of her, because the evidence was there that she had flown up and broke through the deer netting to escape this invisible threat, and now, she was on the loose.

"Why today?" I asked myself. It was raining. I was soaked. And let me tell you, wet jeans are no fun, especially when it's damp outside.

---

[23] This breed from a town called Marans in France is solid black with copper neck feathers. It lays dark chocolate eggs, which are supposedly James Bond's favorite brown egg.

I grabbed a deck brush (yes, the one that I clean chicken coops with) to help me back her into an area to grab her up. I mean, it's easier to catch an escaped chicken with two people, but it's still possible by yourself (though not as easy). So, Estelle, the Black Copper Marans hen, took off, and the game began.

Luckily, chickens are predictable. There are a few things that you should know.

> #1 – Chickens always want to reunite with their flock.
>
> #2 – Chickens will run around and around outside of a pen to accomplish Rule #1.
>
> #3 – Chickens will turn around when confronted with a broom (or deck brush).

Using this knowledge, I proceeded with my deck brush and launched into some thick brush surrounding the pen. In hindsight, I should probably have cut this back long ago, but I figured that each run should have a little privacy from their neighbors, right?

After multiple trips around the pen, because Estelle is fit and fast, this old lady (that's me) finally caught up with her. But then, Estelle used her chicken brain and took a sudden turn and headed down the trail. *Doh!*

Granted, this was unexpected, and against the chicken rules stated above, but I was tired of trying to "run" through thickets, so I was slightly relieved, especially when she ran toward the chicken tractors in a clearing. She was hoping they would let her in, because there is always more safety in numbers.

But using rule #3 above, with my left hand, I extended the deck brush to my left. She faked right, then tried to return left, realized the broom was still there, then returned to the right for real this time. I put my hand down, and she went back to the left, being her only option, as I was behind her, and the chicken tractor was in front of her. As she moved to the left, I kept the deck brush in position to her left and reached down with my right hand...

Success!

I got her by the leg. Dropping the deck brush, I picked her up securely and walked her back home. She had a rough time of it, as the whole ordeal left her looking like a *hot mess*!

As a last ditch effort, she gave one more shot at escaping out of my hands, but there was *no way* I was going to play this game again. I held on for dear life, which is how I got a hand full of feathers from a wet chicken named Estelle.

Now, you might assume that Estelle had learned her lesson. But once an escapee, always an escapee.

A few weeks later, Estelle decided to dig under the fence. I don't mean like a dog who digs under a fence. Oh, no! Chickens are much more covert than that. And a little passive aggressive if you ask me.

"Just taking a dust bath... right next to the fence."

"Oh, that feels so good. I think I'll make a deeper hole."

And suddenly, the chicken has rolled around and right underneath the fence. *Doh*! Of course, they frame complete innocence. "I don't know how in the world that happened. But since I'm outside the fence, I might as well explore the world." And off they go.

While cleaning coops again (the chore that never really ends), I saw Estelle... outside the coop run... again! Having tasted freedom once before, she knew the routine. "Mom is going to chase me around and try to catch me, while I try to elude her." I saw chickens in their runs on each side starting to take bets.

Farmer VS Estelle: Who would win?

As the game started, I noticed the chickens in the other runs were running back and forth with us. Everyone was involved in the "Chicken Olympics". This farm was slowly turning into a funny farm, and I swear it was about to send me into a whole other type of funny farm if this madness continued.

Eventually, I cornered her with the deck brush (remember rule #3). Feeling trapped, she panicked, and that's when, with one swoop, I grabbed her by the legs. She squawked bloody murder with all her might. The other chickens who had bet against me started squawking up a storm too.

"Unfair!" they screamed. "The broom is cheating!"

While holding the mischievous little bugger, I gathered several large sticks to pile against the fence.

Yeah, take that Estelle! You're going to have to start lifting weights to move all those logs.

"Challenge accepted," she cackled back at me.

Now, the key here is that the best method for catching a chicken is to always go for the legs. First, chickens think that they can just hop over your hand and keep going, so they aren't as scared by that as a hand going for their body. Second, feathers can be slick, so grabbing the body doesn't always work, and they can more easily escape again. Third, the legs allow you a firm grip that they can't escape from, which also allows you to carry multiple chickens at once.

And sometimes, you need to catch a chicken for no other reason than dragging them off to Chicken Jail, like Peaches as we'll see next.

LESSONS LEARNED:

- Chickens are predictable. (1) They always want to reunite with their flock. (2) They will run around outside a pen to accomplish #1. (3) Chickens will turn away from a broom.

- Chickens can escape both over a fence and under a fence. When scared, they can fly up and break through deer netting. Or they can dig a hole next to the fence to go under.

- To catch a chicken, always go for the legs. (1) They aren't as scared of a hand going for the legs. (2) Feathers are slick, so it's hard to get a firm hold. (3) Legs offer a firm grip.

Chapter 15

BECOMING A JAIL BIRD

*B*ad Chicks, Bad Chicks,
What ya gonna do? What ya gonna do when they come for you?
Bad Chicks, Bad Chicks.

Seriously, sometimes you just get a rotten egg in the flock. Yep, roosters aren't the only ones that can cause issues. A dominant hen can bully the other hens too. This can happen when you have younger hens that are smaller or when you incorrectly introduce new hens to the group (which you should have learned to do correctly in Chapter 5).

Either way, there's always that *one* hen. In our case, it was Peaches, who had picked up some bad habits from Bertha the Very Mean Chicken. Instead of taking out her aggression on eggs in the nesting box like Bertha, Peaches decided to pluck the feathers out of the other hens for sport.

After all, Peaches was aptly named for her blonde feathers, as she was a Buff Orpington hen, though she was nowhere as beautiful as Gloria from Chapter 11. And I think that is where the problem developed.

Mirror, mirror, on the coop

Who's the prettiest chicken of the group?

Well, apparently Peaches didn't like the answer she got back. And that is when all hell broke loose in the chicken yard, especially toward Gloria. The chickens seemed distraught at dinnertime with a very proud and puffed up Peaches showing her dominance.

Peaches was living her Best Chicken Life at the top of the pecking order, all at the expense of the other chickens. The pecking order is a real thing, and it involves a lot of pecking toward the weaker hens in the flock. Normally, this is nothing to be concerned about, but when there is clearly violence happening, then you as the chicken parent need to introduce Chicken Jail[24].

---

[24] The sometimes necessary means of separating a chicken bully from the rest of the flock in order to reset the pecking order.

I know, I know, this sounds horrible. I mean we already discussed Bertha's mugshot in Chapter 13. Why she hasn't been put away for life behind bars is beyond me. But it was time for Peaches to become a Jail Bird too.

Now, Chicken Jail is a relatively simple concept and easy to implement. You only need a nice size dog crate. Place it in the middle of the Chicken Yard with food and water along with the troublemaker hen. If you have a sick or injured chicken, it's the same thing, except the crate is placed in a safe, quiet area for the injured hen to rest.

In this case, the crate with the hen inside needs to be on full display for the other hens to see. This allows all the other hens to become braver and braver over the next three days, as they approach the crate and aren't attacked by the Jail Bird. And since the instigator can't peck them from the inside of the crate, it reduces the confidence of the Jail Bird. Thus, in three days, the pecking order is reset when the Jail Bird is integrated back into the flock via the steps in Chapter 5.

Now, this worked like a charm for Peaches, and her attitude was adjusted. Of course, Bertha clucked up a storm, as if trying to give Peaches a pep talk, but it was to no avail. And lest you think that this was just a one-off incident. One of our farm family members, Laura, also texted me, though her situation was slightly different.

In her case, a predator had killed all but one of her lovely hens. And this fortunate hen grew to enjoy being a solitary bird with all the pampering and attention being directed solely at her. But Laura had intentions of buying this lone hen some friends as soon as they came available.

The morning Laura arrived was bright and sunny, and they had driven a good distance to pick up their new feathered friends. She oohed and ahhed over the beautiful ladies and could hardly wait to integrate them with her lone hen.

She put the new ladies into the coop at dark as instructed. But the next morning, this lone hen was not having it, as she knew that she should be alone. Like an older child that has a new baby sibling suddenly appear, this lone hen was throwing a tantrum of epic proportions and taking out all her frustrations on the poor younger hens who were at a complete loss at what they had done wrong to deserve this in their new home.

I received a text from a distraught Laura, asking what she should do to correct this issue. The answer was Chicken Jail. Once the lone hen was placed in a crate in the middle of the chicken yard, it really took the wind right out of her sails. The younger hens became braver, and even seemed to taunt her by day three.

Once this lone hen was released from Chicken Jail, the attitude adjustment was complete, and she accepted her new siblings, though maybe not with complete fondness. However, they were able to co-exist, which is sometimes the best that we can ask for when Chicken Jail is needed.

LESSONS LEARNED:

- Chicken Jail can be used for both roosters or hens, depending on the situation. It is used to stop bullying and reset the pecking order.

- A large dog crate can be used for the chicken jail. Keep out of direct sun. Make sure that the bottom is covered with straw and has room for food and water.

- The pecking order is usually reset within three days, and then the Jail Bird can be reintroduced to the flock via the steps in Chapter 5.

Is this Good-bye?

t's always sad when you come to the end of a book where you just loved all the stories. So, if you're craving more stories like the ones in this book, be sure to join our email list for daily farm stories and educational content.

Go to: www.HendricksFarmMcBeanGA.com
to sign up and join our farm family.

P.S. Remember—every Friday is a new Chicken Chat video, where we cluck about all things chicken.

Find us on YouTube, Facebook, and Instagram @HendricksFarmMcBeanGA.

Looking to Heal Your Body with Food?

was too! And the issue I found was that even so-called healthy organic meats were pumped full of antibiotics or fed a soy and corn based diet.

It was so frustrating. My body was wasting away, and my hair was falling out. And every time I tried to eat something, I suffered agonizing abdominal pain.

Then, I learned that 99.9% of all animal feed is made up of Soy and Corn. And studies have shown that what an animal eats will end up in the meat and eggs that you consume.

And yes, I was having reactions to meat and eggs due to the soy in them. Thus, I became a vegan for almost a decade. I was down to fruits, vegetables, and nuts.

Then, one day, I wondered if I could raise a better chicken, so that I wouldn't have a reaction anymore. And thus began the adventure of starting my own farm.

Today, Hendricks Farm has won the prestigious "Best of Georgia" award for two consecutive years, and we ship our frozen meats to the 48 contiguous states of the United States.

- 100% Grass-Fed *and* Grass-Finished Beef
- Pasture-Raised Chickens with No Soy, Corn, or other junk
- Pasture-Raised Turkeys—coming Fall 2024
- Pasture-Raised Pork—coming Fall 2024

My personal mission is to provide the healthiest meats, on dare I say the entire planet. If I can't eat it, I don't sell it. Period.

Sign up for our daily emails at
www.HendricksFarmMcBeanGA.com.

Acknowledgements

T hank you to Ricardo Mossini from Argentina for the incredible drawings in this book. You can find him on Fiverr @ricardomossini7. I highly recommend him.

To Emily Kamala, my first business coach, who saw things in me that I couldn't see at the time and continued to push me forward in my business. Forever grateful for our friendship.

To Jenn Lowe, who has been the most reliable and trustworthy friend anyone could ask for. You are truly a badass in the best way possible. Thank you for helping me when I needed it.

To Linh Valory, who has been a true friend and has graciously driven across the street many times to help in times of need on our farm, always with a smile on her beautiful face.

To Mitizi Sayler, who is the most amazing chicken momma and has been a tremendous help out at our farm. She is the most uplifting person you'll ever meet.

To Sandy Cleveland, who always supported and encouraged me and still is my biggest cheerleader.

To Mrs. D., the brave soul who successfully tamed her Cock in Chapter 10. She was one of our first farm family members and has since become a good friend over the years.

To Ed Duvall, who was the first customer to say that I needed to write a book with all my chicken stories that I sent to my email list.

To Bob Arvizu, who I worked with for nearly 10 years in the IT industry. He always told me that I had a gift for writing, and he just loved the way I told stories. I'm heartbroken that he recently passed before he could see my first published book.

To my Mom, who spent hours reading to me when I was little and made our weekly Saturday trip to the library such a highlight of my life that I was bound to grow up and write a book myself. I hope that you find this book to be an enjoyable read.

To my Granddad and Grandma Jacobs, who are no longer here with us. The memories made on your farm each summer will live in my heart forever. I wish that I had spent more time learning about how you raised your chickens, but your warning about using an iron-clad glove lives with me forever, as discussed in Chapter 13.

And to the person (they know who they are) who would be embarrassed if I put their name in a Chicken Book of all things, but who actively listened to all my fowl stories nonetheless and encouraged me to reach for the stars.

And last but certainly not least, all my farm family members who have read my daily emails and responded to me with encouraging words and helpful suggestions. You have become dear friends to me, and I feel blessed to have you in my life. Thank you for coming on this journey with me!

About the Author

Jenny M. Hendricks always enjoyed traveling every summer from her hometown of Lubbock, Texas, to her grandparent's farm in Felt, Oklahoma right across the state line. Even with all the experiences at her grandparents' farm every summer, she never thought she would actually own chickens when she grew up to be an adult.

After graduating as Valedictorian, she obtained Summa Cum Laude from Texas Tech University in just three years while also working full-time at Red Lobster. Who knew that learning to handle live lobsters with deadly claws would come in handy later in life? While working a professional job, she went on to obtain a Master's of Science in Computer Information Systems from University of Phoenix.

After years spent hacking away at the computer of various Information Technology consulting jobs, her health took a sudden turn for the worse. She had lost so much weight that you could see the bones in her body, and her hair had started falling out too. After much research, she determined that it was her diet causing the issue. But even eating healthier didn't fully heal her until she determined that it was the soy being fed to animals that was causing her reaction to meat and other foods, which contained this soy.

She became a Certified Master Gardener in Michigan and started growing her own vegetables, including 200 pounds of potatoes per year, which she stored in the cool basement. Later, she moved back down South to Georgia, and she started raising her own chickens on Non-Gmo, Soy-Free, Corn-Free, and Non-Medicated feed. It truly made a huge difference in her health, and other people started taking notice.

Today, her farm has won the prestigious "Best of Georgia" award every year that they have officially been in business, and they are currently shipping their frozen meats to all 48 states. She writes daily emails to her ever-growing farm family email list about animal stories or educational content. Her mission is to help others on their health journey, whether that is providing them directly with healthy meats or educating them on homesteading for them to be more self-sufficient.

Sign up for her daily emails at
www.HendricksFarmMcBeanGA.com.

Could you do me a Personal Favor please?

First, let me say a big TEXAS-sized THANK YOU for reading my first published book. Seriously, I'm honored that you read my book.

Now, it's always sad when you come to the end of a book where you just loved all the stories. But why not share your love of this book with another person by leaving an Amazon Review?

Would you please take two minutes *right now* to leave a helpful review on Amazon? I love reading all the feedback, as it helps me to continue to improve.

Oh yeah, Bertha the Very Mean Chicken says it better be a 5 Star Review or she'll peck your eye out. She might be serious. It's really hard to say what mood she's in at the moment.

Thanks again for cluckin' around with all of us out here at the farm. It's been a shell of a time!

Jenny

Made in United States
Orlando, FL
30 November 2024

54615172R00085